Know that you
yourself are a Miracle.

Dr. Norman Vincent Peale

AF342364

Happy Birthday Beautiful
Loving Sister of mine.....

2010

poems of
the hidden way

To my grandchildren:

Gregory and Nelly, Marc,
Daniel, Michael, Matthew,
David, Karen, Michael,
and Christopher

Catherine de Vinck

poems of
the hidden way

Alleluia Press

By the same author:
A Time to Gather, 1967, 1974, 1987
Ikon, 1972, 1974 (O.P.)
A Liturgy, 1973, 1974, 1977
A Passion Play, 1975
A Book of Uncommon Prayers, 1977, 1978 (O.P.)
Readings (John at Patmos & A Book of Hours), 1978
A Book of Eve (LP Record & Text), 1979
A Garland of Straw, 1981
A Book of Peace, 1985
News of the World in Fifteen Stations, 1988

Library of Congress Catalogue Card Number: 91-76162
Published by ALLELUIA PRESS, Allendale, NJ 07401
Printed and bound in the United States of America
ISBN 0-911726-53-5
Cover illustration: *The Tree of Light or Blazing Tree,* Hannah Cahoon 1845
    Facsimile reproduction of original at Hancock Shaker Village

CONTENTS

FOREWORD

For those already familiar with the work of Catherine de Vinck, no further introduction is necessary. We learn to await rich fare from her heart and her pen, and we are not disappointed. For those encountering her poetry here for the first time, the resonances and power of her finely crafted words will be the most adequate of introductions. You, the reader, are invited to a personal engagement with the poet, to a moment of encounter and dialogue in which each is an active participant.

"Without vision, the people perish," an ancient Hebrew writer stated, expressing the enduring vocation of the poet: to be a person "with far-seeing eyes," committed to the life-work of shaping and sharing a vision of the present and the future, in the midst of the human community. The poet protests the lack of vision, a famine which brings only a harvest of death. Catherine de Vinck is such a woman of vision.

But *which* vision will guide us? The horrors of this century teach us that a skewed and distorted vision can equally bring death to the world. The hallmark of this Age of Ideologies is the endless list of vanquished nations and subjugated peoples, a succession of "world orders" unable to break free from the spiral of violence, the cancerous stockpiling of the weapons of mass destruction. In such times, the poet's vocation is to be a person of *critical* vision. She fashions images and metaphors strong and shocking enough to unmask the empty promises that rob us of our humanity, that steal the future from our children. And once our eyes are opened, she invites us to the loom of life, to weave with her a transfigured world destined for peace, communion, and justice, a world in which tenderness and hope are safe. Catherine de Vinck is such a poet of critical vision.

In *Poems of the Hidden Way*, this critical, healing vision unfolds: nourished by the waters of ancient wisdom, rooted in the ever-new poem of the Beatitudes, grounded in empathy with creation's struggle for peace, and animated by an irrepressible hope. It is not only the vision of Catherine de Vinck that is extraordinary in the nuclear age, but also the way in which she has singularly embraced our common human journey. These pages reveal a woman who has learned -- from her own experience of love, motherhood, suffering, loss, and hope -- how to perceive reality through the eyes of those who hunger for bread, who suffer the ravages of war, who work tirelessly for a world without weapons. The life and death of her son Oliver, and the lives and deaths of the innocent in war, are linked in the most profound way. Her poems remind us that each of us, none excepted, is called to develop such a *universal* heart.

These poems are not simply texts, but an *event*, a living encounter between the poet and the reader/hearer. They are, therefore, especially suited for those privileged moments of prayer and silence, during which we enter into the divine vision for the world, and deepen our commitment to the living of that vision. In a time when traditional religious language often fails to awaken us to the Holy Mystery in which we are immersed, these poems offer a rich resource of images and metaphors for naming both the God of Peace, and ourselves, in personal and public prayer.

For twenty years, the Benedictine monastic community of Weston Priory has feasted at the table of Catherine de Vinck's poetry. Her artistry has quietly, gently taken its place in the brothers' personal and communal prayer. So too will this latest collection, which reminds us that

> *(w)e can still make it*
>> gather the threads, the pieces
> each of different size and shade
>> to match and sew into a pattern...
> The coming of night will be darker
>> than the heart of stones
> *unless we strike the match*
>> *light the guiding candle*
>> say, "Yes, there is room after all
>>> at the inn."[1]

Catherine de Vinck lights the guiding candle in these pages, a healing vision for humankind's entrance into the twenty-first century. We trust that, like the brothers of Weston, many others will discover both encouragement and inspiration in her exceptional gift.

> The Benedictine Monks of Weston Priory
> Weston, Vermont, U.S.A.
> 1991

[1] *from the poem "A Time for Everything," in this collection. Italics ours.*

I

the beatitudes

THE BEATITUDES

Blessed are the poor in spirit,
    for theirs is the kingdom of heaven.
Blessed are the meek,
    for they shall possess the earth.
Blessed are they who mourn,
    for they shall be comforted.
Blessed are they who hunger and thirst for justice,
    for they shall be satisfied.
Blessed are the merciful,
    for they shall obtain mercy.
Blessed are the pure of heart,
    for they shall see God.
Blessed are the peacemakers,
    for they shall be called the children of God.
Blessed are they who suffer persecution for justice' sake,
    for theirs is the kingdom of heaven.

BLESSED ARE THE POOR IN SPIRIT,
FOR THEIRS IS THE KINGDOM
OF HEAVEN.

Poured out
> from one cup to another
> words spill and splash.
Their liquid selves
> - bright rosy wine of language -
poured out
> from lip to lip
> from meaning to meaning
to say what?
> Poor and blessed in odd coupling.

Are we poor
> when we stand at time's gate
> ragged beggars asking
> for the cheap clanging of pity
> for the change of dime-store feelings?

What we learn in the dark
> in cellar rooms and closets
what is whispered to us
> in steep descending stairs
what we learn in the shadows
> - shame and guilt mingling
> with the scent of stale air -
takes us closer to mental places
> of poverty and want.

To speak of reality, we name
        the orange on the table
        the bed with flowered sheets
        the immediate warmth of a wrist
        pressed with fingertips, held to feel
        the sonorous heart beating
        in its rich central cave.
We have not left Egypt, not yet:
        olives and grapes fill our dish
        the pots are simmering on alien fires.
We play the guitar, sing at our feasts
        declare our collective sin
        by passing the plate
        dropping the dollar bills
        for distant starving children.

Contained behind frontiers and fences
        the hungry look on, observe
huge ledgers propped on stone tables
        see the columns of ciphers swelling
        into colossal useless sums.
In parched fields
        the eyeless skulls of cattle stare
        white and hard out of hollow sockets.
In the cities
        the faces of the poor appear, disappear
        in the smoke of sacrifices.
They live downhill, downwind
        their odor cannot reach
        our balconies and gardens.
We are spring and summer
        to their shivering winter;
we are horns of plenty
        fulsome baskets and bowls;
they are grey emptiness
        husks and straws
        swept away by careless brooms.

All is not lost:
        there is a God walking the land.
His voice a clap
        in the bell of the world
rings out:
        justice, liberation, peace.

He, without origin or ancestor
        wedges his splendor between history's walls
housing himself, a child in a womanly space
        to become God of the byways
descending through the stairs of his mercy
        into the black holes of despair
to say, "All is not lost!
        Your emptiness curves out
        into a vase of bright lips
        open, infinitely open for gifts
        for the poured libation of blessings."

When we gather and reap
        do we have anything in mind
other than storing, other than building
        bigger barns and better locks?
Do we know
        the Witness rages against us
        sets an angel with twirling sword
        to guard the tree of universal summer
        against us, predators, despoilers
        killers of stillness, of peace?

What do we own
        when the clasp of our life
        loosens and breaks?
No recourse
        but to find the narrow road
the thin line through bramble and brush
        where God walks ahead of us

more houseless than the fox
poorer than the mouse in its grassy nest.

Dreams, nostalgia, cherished thoughts:
we fold the painted cloth
we shed the mantle belled with stars.
How pleasant the ringing of our name
in market place and street!
We bend neck and knee
fall silent within the immense silence
where all sounds end their flight.
Our naked hands lie quiet, empty
in the lap of nothingness.
Our mind undresses, leaves its garments
- vibrant scarlet, sequined gold -
to dip in the dark pool of pure night
of an ignorance deeper than knowledge.
At the place of absolute need
we find, receive, the cup of benediction
full
overflowing.

BLESSED ARE THE MEEK,
FOR THEY SHALL POSSESS THE EARTH.

A distant province
        beyond familiar boundaries
an empty space
        beyond habitual containment
        of fence or retaining wall:
nothing there
        only moving sand, angular rocks
        and the pliant, frenzied wind
        twirling itself hot.

Meekness lives here
        a slender figure
walking unharmed among lions and jackals.
Her tent is pitched on burnished ground
        under a sun, fierce and African
        in its ardor and heat.
Her face is naked
        in the dance of masks;
her hands plunge
        into jars of grain;
her body's musical range
        out-beats the sound
        of barbaric drums.

Armies are on the move:
        any number can play.
The most exalted shall win favor

shall raise golden standards
        to announce the coming reign
            of the slain.
Within the trampled furrow
        seeds shrivel, tender shoots die
        crushed and soiled.
In a fire of thorns, the lamb burns
        its flesh darkening to ashes.
She walks the battlefields
        lady of oil and linen
bending over wounds that scream
        hate, despair.
She is a sealed fountain
        breaking open
a spirit of water
        immaculately poured.
Arrested for trespassing
        pushed into vans
        chained ankle to ankle
        wrist to wrist
she lies bruised and still
        releasing her pure fragrance
        before soldier and judge.

Hers is the outreach of the land
        the spiral flight through infinite skies
        beyond the prison walls.
Hers is the absolute ground:
        knowledge in the night of ignorance
        beauty in the face of terror
        peace in a time of war.
Lightly, she taps us on the shoulder:
        she is that slight touch
felt now and then at odd moments;
        she is that puzzling summons:
when we answer

holding our guttering candle
        to her strong and steady light
she leads us by ascending stairs
        to the throne-room of the world.
What do we find there?
        Life
this daily commonplace life
        woven of necessity and want
newly discovered, recognized
        as a fulsome text, all words included
all languages understood, all voices
        rising in a concert to sing
        HOLY HOLY HOLY
        the Name of the nameless God.

BLESSED ARE THEY WHO MOURN,
FOR THEY SHALL BE COMFORTED.

All night long
    the women invent new patterns
    weave new cloth:
somber, the color of ashes,
    the grey of spider webs and dust.
They wrap themselves in sounds
    low, muffled, in which they turn
    return, roll themselves as in sheets.

All night long
    the moths come to the flame
    sizzling their wings, falling
    in soft heaps around the lamps.

No one sleeps.
    Death walks under the moon
    slides under doorsills
    slips through cracks in the walls.
No one sleeps.
    The women weep
bound each to each by the long strips
    tumbling from their looms in dark folds.
They are weaving plant fibers
    elements outdating the work of machines
    the rhythmical clicking in factories and mills.

This is real flesh beaten and wounded;
    these are real hands lifted to the sky;

these are bodies keening
        by the altar stone
- mouths without appetite
        eyes with no other sight
        than unmasked dread.
These are minds which suddenly understand
        ancient words of pasture and shepherd;
these are ears listening to calls
        to voices faintly heard in the distance
        speaking of comfort, of peace.

What can be said
        when the child is laid out
        thin and silent in a white robe?
What can be said
        when on the other side of summer
the frozen corpse floats under the ice
        a slow cargo laced with water vines
        descending into its water tomb?
What can be said
        when the trembling boy is caught
        roped, carried to alien shores?
When the young girl
        in her delicate bones
rides the great moans of her mother
        embarks on the Egyptian boat
        spelling underground doom?

Where is the Comforter, the one who brings
        brew of forgetfulness
        blue smoke of oceanic dreams?
Nameless, he comes at dawn
        when the sun loudly lifts
        its modulations of golden tones.
He comes after the long night:
        balm of lily and rose

potent wine poured forth
from the pure star in the East.

What does he say, what answers
    the old massive questions
    of grief without respite
    death without end?
Only a single word:
        Himself
    light of lights
    who comes down from heaven
    in a real body
to die, to rise every day
    defining the limits of sorrow
    repealing the edicts of death.

BLESSED ARE THEY WHO HUNGER
AND THIRST FOR JUSTICE,
FOR THEY SHALL BE SATISFIED.

Imagine a great house:
    underfoot, the steadiness of marble
    the smooth polish of stone.
Along the wall
    the letters of the law stand guard
black scripted, angular, shaped
    like ancient weapons, lances, swords.
In cold anterooms, they are waiting
    men, women wrapped in blankets and shawls.
They are hungry, they thirst: in their dreams
    justice means oat cakes and milk
    spoons dipped in full platters
a bed sheeted with clean linen
    oil for skillet and lamp.
The poor murmur among themselves
    their speech rich with pauses
    with thoughts slowly decanted
    into small cups of words.

"We have come," they say
    "through tunnels and mazes.
We have traveled underground:
    our hands are mapped with labor
    our bodies are bruised.
We limp from long falls
    down the stairs of affliction.
All we know of history lies crumpled

in newspapers stuffed
    between spidery cracks
    in broken window panes.
We are in danger:
    violence stabs our mind
urges us to take to the hills
    to write a new theology of freedom
    outside rules and prescriptions.
We have come in peace
    believing in possibilities:
a life sewn from the whole cloth
    lovingly embroidered with temporal scenes
    of shelter and food."

Often, they are sent away
    to re-enter airless rooms
configurations of the mind
    where all exits are blocked.
They do not understand:
    a lifelong patience
is not enough to grasp
    the function of the functionary
    the scribbling of the scribe
    all the sentences passed
    to separate, to tear, to strip.

Shall the Word breathe
    through the silence and the darkness?
Shall the exiles be called
    from their Egypt of servitude
to a land buzzing with bees
    flowing with rivers of milk?

    Believe!
Women will conceive, bring forth
    new ways of seeing, of touching

of being alive and free.
Out of ancient lore, men will retrieve
        scraps of ancient rituals
melodies of lost languages
        earth-music
energies of rain and sun
        working in unison
to raise water in the wells
        corn in the fields.
Children will break into a dance
        will break-dance, break-fast in the streets
and justice - blessed be she -
        having traveled through arid places
having despaired, having been trapped
        in deep pits of abstraction
will dwell in the neighborhood
        a familiar figure, a good mother
        baker of bread
        dispenser of equal portions.

BLESSED ARE THE MERCIFUL,
FOR THEY SHALL OBTAIN MERCY.

asy
      to pull the blanket
      to cover the naked drunkard.
Easy
      to forgive the trespasser
      snatcher of purse and ring.
Easy
      to lift the flask to dying lips
      - the enemy propped up
      against a pillar of history
      defeated.

Lazy mercy, easy mercy
      gathering flowers for the dead
      in a meadow ablaze with wild lilies.
She hums to herself, fills her basket
      mother of mercy, plump and easy
      walking in clover.

When the eye looks further
      beyond the safety of house and fence
words hang in the air
      red frozen screams
enormously suspended from winter trees
      where crows assemble.
There are no yesterdays, no tomorrows
      in the murderous chronicles:

lynching   genocide   pogrom
        private cruelty, public abuse
the newsreel turns, speeded up
        past, present and future merge
in a single immense blur
        a dark stain, impossible to blot.
Not to be ignored:
        lapses, betrayals, compromises
        sly complicities.
Do we observe our own battle-zones
        in the grey stretches of our soul?

                O mother of mercy
deliver us from the furies
        shrieking for revenge;
remove us from the context
        of our violence, of our anger.
Too much, we know too much:
        only a gauzy veil of time hangs
between us and those who wait
        under whip and club to board the train
that forever circles the globe
        with its cargo of pain.

How do we respond to the ashes
        snowing in brittle flakes
        on the ordinary objects of the day?
How do we stop the wailing
        of our brothers and sisters
seated by the embers of the great wars?

"Love your enemy.
        Bless, do not curse.
                Create, do not destroy.
                        Love, do not hate."

Bring us forth into the light
        mother mercy, mother courage
and by the rose-candle of compassion
        give us voice to say:
"Forgive us our trespasses
        as we forgive those
                who trespass against us."
Amen, amen, alleluia!

BLESSED ARE THE PURE OF HEART,
FOR THEY SHALL SEE GOD.

Let it go:
>   ornament, disguise, mask;
throw away the hats and cloaks
>   the wool pulled over the eyes;
yank from the windows
>   the heavy drapes that obscure
>   obstruct the rising light.
Dawn tints the sky:
>   time to drag yourself out of bed
>   to let the dreams snow out of your head.
Their tiny feathers are no match
>   for the sturdy morning birds
>   the brown sparrows twittering
>   in the pine by the back door.

Why do you fear open spaces?
You cannot meet anyone but yourself
>   daughter of the moon
>   son of the stars
nightwalkers darkly traveling
>   up and down the mountain of your sleep
notching the stones as you pass
>   with runes, with diagrams of memories.
To remember, to be remembered
>   you collect shells, china cups, notebooks
keep old clothes hanging for decades
>   in closet and attic
like dried skins powdered with age.

Break the spell!
The objects of this room
        are not to be trusted:
convoluted machinery of the clock
        damask chair, leather purse
they are the contraband smuggled
        into your life in a time of hunger.
Helpless, benumbed
        you sit in their midst
while the flux of their energy wanes
        under rust and rot
leaving gaps in your world
        black holes of emptiness and want.

Enough, enough! It is time
        to vacate the ancient house
tear down fences and barricades
        all that separates word from word
        noun from verb
        ordinary voice from song.

There are many roads, byways, paths
        to the heart of the matter
but unless you wake
you'll continue to sleepwalk
to miss the sight of the sun-flower
        opening its immense petals
        calling you to enter its immense light.

"There is nothing since the beginning,"
        said Thoreau
        "but the eye and the sun."
Through the eye, reality increases
        doubles itself, repeats as in a mirror
        the face, the tree, the wing of the moth.
Scar, bruise, wart, do they appear

enlarged on that watery screen
or does inner/outer correspond
        in exact symmetry, each to each
like twin valves of a shell
        hinged into fitted replicas
        at all points of contact?

The eye alone does not see:
        on its lens
images print themselves
        in fast succession, careless of meaning.
Behind the eye stands the witness
        filing the sequences into orderly texts:
there, white fields of winter
impressionistic landscape
        with crows and dried weeds;
here, table, dish, vase with tulips
        map of the ordinary
        sequel of dailiness.

"If the doors of perception were cleansed,"
        said Blake
"everything would appear as it is
        infinite."

        Time to wake up
to enter far enough, deep enough
        into your heart.
The path is cluttered
        by the rubble of many years
defended by raging beasts
        by shadows fingering you
        with phantom-grey hands.

Never mind:
        descend, ascend

into that living breathing place.
Then you will begin to see
        by way of water, fire, earth and air
        by way of love for all beings
see within/beyond, no-where/every-where
        as through a glass darkly
                the faceless face of God.

BLESSED ARE THE PEACEMAKERS,
FOR THEY SHALL BE CALLED
CHILDREN OF GOD.

Now all we are doing
        is to stand on railroad tracks
barring the way to the train
        that carries our future:
canisters of plutonium
        containers of radiant plagues
        of tumors without remission
        of winters without end.
Destination: living flesh.

All we are doing
        is to stumble through the desert
form a circle, pray hand in hand:
        "Deliver us from this manner of death
from the terror blossoming
        into a parasol of fire over our heads;
deliver us from masters in black boots
        from uniforms that hide the particular:
        delicate shading of skin
        diversity of thoughts."

We are pushed into vans
        handcuffed
branded as trouble-makers
        by armed trouble-shooters
        in a time of war.

All we are doing
        is to open a door
a soft door shaped like a womb
        opening to give birth
        to mercy and compassion.
Through that portal, refugees pass
        peasants chased from their high sierras
        by soldiers, policemen, torturers
while the tranquil faces of landlords
        are reflected in gilded mirrors
        in pacific waters
        where the drowned float.

We have arrived at these places
        slowly, reading instructions
following a filigree of tangled lines
        roads on the map of danger and exile.

The facts enter the mind
        needle-sharp
press on nerve cells
        activate the concept: peace.
We begin to feel life
        pliant, womanly, tender
instead of ironclad, armor-plated
        wounding and wounded.
We begin to imagine
        family trees springing up
        green and sturdy
growing without loss
        their branches intertwined
        supporting one another.

    Peace:
in all pantries and cupboards
        bags of lentils and rice
        sacks of sugar and flour;

posies in the hands of children
        valentines, hearts and ribbons
        in all the mailboxes of the world.

        Peace:
        to be!
For each thing to be
        according to its own code:
filament, fiber, molecular thread
        spun into fragile marginal creatures.
What right for the spider and the sparrow?
        What purpose to the snail inching its way
        along its moisture trail?
Should the ant be crushed
        under the stamping foot?
Should the tiger end up
        skinned on the palace floor?
Should the earth-mother
        be stripped and shorn
        her garments ripped
        her good brown body slashed
        her generous teats cut off?

Let it be
        let it be in our caring
        touched, caressed, held
that soft nest, feathers and moss
        where we as fledglings
break out of the blue cosmic egg.

Peace:
a woman of uncommon mind
        seated among her sisters.
Between them, a shuttle of good words
        weaves a new language of strength.
        A man who had a dream:
"To rise from the dark and desolate valley

of segregation;
to be free at last!"
	A man who said:
"We must not allow our creative protest
	to degenerate into physical violence.
Again and again, we must rise
	to the majestic heights
of meeting physical violence
	with soul force."

	A grasshopper of a man
fasting in far-off India saying:
"Suffering injury in one's own person
	is of the essence of non-violence
and is the chosen substitute
	for violence to others."

	A woman running through
	the black tunnel of slavery
to emerge at the head of the bus
	calm, unafraid, wearing freedom
	a fresh rose pinned to her dress.

	Children
they shall be called
	children of blessings
those who walk unarmed
	in a world glittering
	with knives and guns.
They shall take notice:
	in the midst of winter
	in lands locked by hate and sorrow
they shall hear now and then
	a little water-song
	clear-cutting the dark silence.
They shall bend down, cup their hands
	in wonder, they shall drink.

BLESSED ARE THEY WHO SUFFER
PERSECUTION FOR JUSTICE' SAKE,
FOR THEIRS IS THE KINGDOM
OF HEAVEN.

Kali Yuga:
        time without beginning
        time of the end.
The old myths, the ancient clues
        no longer provide shelter
        against the assembled shadows:
black-caped, masked, nameless
        dance macabre on the world's stage.

Kali Yuga:
        voices of prisoners
        fill the space
        occupied yesterday by innocent objects
        by word-containers of bread and milk.
In the torturer's chamber
        human figures are cut up
the pieces reformed, Picasso-like
        in a collage that distorts
        convulses eyes and mouths.

What have they done
        those who weep, snowed under
in a Siberia of icy grieving
        their feet in straw
        their speech, grunts and howls?

What have they done
        those with broken hands
descending stone-heavy
        into water-depths of pain?
        Women on the road
driving home in a land of sorrow:
        ambushed, raped, shot
the imprint of their lives
        forever stamped on the rock of this age.
They are continuing their journey
        moving now in lightness of being
entering language, stories, books
        their names written down
        burned on the pages
flashing their luminous sequences:
        Maura, Ita, Dorothy, Jean.

Who dares to speak
        to let the truth explode
        in the market square
where slaves pull heavy carts
        display their wares:
their lives coiled in clay
        baked into fragile pots:
a knock, a push, a kick
        and they break.
He breaks with them
        Oscar Romero
killed in San Salvador:
        his blood forever flows
freshly pools at the tyrants' feet
        wherever they step
        out of their limousines
on the way to yet another execution.

Mothers, sisters, lovers
        they stand in the nightmare

adjusting verb and noun to fit
         the description of the disappeared.
They are last testaments
         scribbled at night
in the most extreme north of their soul
         where syllables freeze, turn
         into piercing crystal thorns.

         Mud-splattered, bloodied
they move through the underground
         midwives mediating birth
pulling refugees across rivers and swamps
         toward sanctuary, a precarious freedom.

Crying in the wilderness
         no enchanted prince he
but a squat brown man
         spat upon, clubbed, jailed
he speaks his Indian mind
         seeking simple things:
clean water in clean cups
         decent housing, fair wages
         for his brothers and sisters
toiling in vineyards and fields:
         Cesar Chavez
child of God, heir to the kingdom.

Light, invisible light
         streams over and above these people
defiers of evil social contracts
         rebels, martyrs
         stretched out in long crucifixions
         for justice' sake.
They grow bright
         brighter than stars in the heavens
for their eyes have seen the glory of the Lord.

II

peace cantata

*Commissioned in 1984 by Regis College (Weston, MA)
with the assistance of a New Works Grant from the
Massachusetts Council on the Arts and Humanities.
Music for organ, brass, tympani, narrators and chorus
composed by Emma Lou Diemer.
Premiered at Regis College, April 18 1986
under the direction of Sheila Pritchard Vogt.*

PEACE CANTATA

In the beginning was the Word
        Word of peace
        spelled in syllables
        of water and earth
        fire and air
        rising like music
through the roots of all things
        composing this planet
        into a place of history
        house of open doors
        space fit for living.

In the beginning
        in time's first turn and shift
man, woman, apart and together
        found intonation, voice
        to name the wonder
        of stone and light and wind.

Later
there was a village, a neighborhood
        people clustered in small rooms
        sharing food, holding in common
        language and lore
        following the roll and pitch
        of sea and moon.

Not all at once, but slowly
        pulling threads of coarse fiber

with needles of bone
    through the scraps of centuries
they pieced together a legacy of sorts, a wisdom
    translated into customs, emblems, rituals
    carried from age to age
    saying:
    "We are more than our pain
    more than the sum of our cravings:
we are thought, dream, perception
    we are song
    in tune with the humming stars
    with the sun's luminous throbbing.

More than on grain and meat
    we feed on mysteries:
    gestures of love
    intimations, hints
    of what it is to be real, to be free
    in a world where all things breathe
    as one great body, serene and motherly.

Now, wherever we look
    there is disaster:
    the hot imprint of fear
    smoking on the flesh.
Lost is our dream
    of simple phrases
    backyards full of children
    chimes ringing golden hours
    that could never be stopped.
It is late: time shrivels, contracts
    to a single black dot
    winds itself down
    to a slackened pulsing."

"Wait," we say

"we can wait a little longer
we can linger and pretend
life is but a silver stream
on which to row our boat
our precious private ark
        gently, safely
out of sight, out of reach."

————

Now, the drumbeat of language
counts profits, programs facts:
        mega-dollars
        mega-bombs
        mega-deaths.
Isn't everybody doing it?
Selling by the pound, by the hour
by the time we reach the docks
where tall ships are bringing in
        coffee and slaves?
Isn't everybody doing it?
        Marketing, buying
        the lives of those who labor
        in cane fields, in tea plantations
        those who weave basket and cloth
        those who scrape the desert floor
        for crumbs fallen from our table?
                "PEACE, PEACE, PEACE"
        we chant in the early dawn.
The words fall like snow
        settle in public places
        but they freeze on the ground
as the clanging of cymbals increases
        announcing death-without-end.

Oh, say, can you see

the plague in the well
the rot in the landfill
the chained barrels in the sea?

Oh, say, can you see
    Guernica, Auschwitz, Babi-Yar
    Rome burning, Jerusalem sacked
    Troy the fallen
    lying broken under the sand?

And, before that
    the striking fist
    the hurled rock
    Abel bleeding in the field?

Oh, say, can you see
    all the nameless places
    nameless people
    ground like stone
    returned to gravel piles
        to lime pits?

Who shall tell us
    the shape of time to come
    if our days are no more
    than a fluttering of wing
    a brief pulsing in the air?
Who shall bring us
    beyond the darkening zone
    of no corn, no apple
    no man's, no woman's land?

What will happen
    if the text of our story blurs
    on the page of creation
    leaving no trace in the radioactive ash?

At every juncture of history
        armies are on the march.
Can we be heard above the din
        above the roar of time spiraling
        down the ages
        turning from dust to dust?

It is late:
        four minutes to midnight
        if we dare to look at the clock.
The weight of darkness bends us
        to the ground of our weeping.
We kneel
        at the gates of deserted houses
        at the border of no-trespassing;
we kneel
        before our brothers and sisters.
Touching the hem of their garments
        we ask forgiveness:
Sand Creek, Wounded-Knee, Mylai!
        We ask forgiveness
        Nagasaki, Hiroshima:
a hundred thousand killed
        by a single bomb
a hundred thousand
        injured or missing!
We ask forgiveness
        we kneel in the cinders
                we beg for mercy.

————

Again and again, we wonder:
        what more can we do?
The echo of the question returns to us
        thinned to a needle of sound

and we are pricked, we are stained
        with the blood of our anguish
            of our doubt.

We may have another year
        we may have a minute or two:
who knows when the calendar will melt
        into a blank space
        a place of no witness
        no mother or father
        no lover or friend
no tree shining with a green light
        no stone left unturned
        no fragment of a word
        left to say, "Love!"
        to name innocence and mercy.

————

In deep silos of fear
        the bombs rest, shining eggs
        laid in the underground
        ready to hatch
        to release their plagues.

It is time to rise
        to free the long scream
        trapped for decades in our throats.
It is time to shout:
        "STOP!"
        Stop the obscene breeding
        the maggots implanted in our soil!
Stop the magicians, the yea-sayers
        stop the lullabies they hum
        to put our vigilance at rest.

What is left to us?
To invent a new story
        a new way
        of being on this earth,
        of being together
forming one luminous body
        one sacred flesh
        smooth, healthy
without remembrance of scars.

———

Pilgrims of space
        we walk on the moon
        wander among numberless mysteries.
Yet our home is here, is now
        in the lands outspread around us
        in widening arcs of color:

AMERICA, AFRICA, ASIA
EUROPE, OCEANIA, ANTARCTICA
        ALL
        linked like syllables of one text
        like voices responding each to each
        distinct, yet equally sustained
                in the one same song.

It is time
        to honor our common work
        to choose light over darkness
                love over hate
                peace over war.
It is time to honor our bodies
to set warm flesh against the destroyers
        to say, "NO! You shall not pass!"

You shall not trespass
        on the holy ground of our living.
You shall not tear the seamless robe
        you shall not kill the child
        neither in the womb
        nor on some foreign street.

It is time to ring the bells
        to announce a seventh day of rest
        a Sun-Day of celebration.

———

We can still make it
        gather the threads, the pieces
        each of different size and shade
        to match and sew into a pattern:
                Rose of Sharon
                Wedding Ring
                Circles and Crowns.

We can still listen
        to children at play
        their voices mingling
        in the present tense
        of a time that can be extended.

"Peace," we say
        looking through our pockets
        to find the golden word
        the coin to buy that ease
        that place sheltered
        from bullets and bombs.

But what we seek lies elsewhere
        beyond the course of lethargic blood

beyond the narrow dream
of resting safe and warm.

If we adjust our lenses
        we see far in the distance
        figures of marching people
        homeless, hungry, going nowhere.
Why not call them
        to our morning of milk and bread?

The coming night will be darker
        than the heart of stone
        unless we strike the match
        light the guiding candle
        say, "Yes, there is room after all
                at the inn."

———

Listen!
        Even in the dark
        the leaves make a green sound:
        even in silence
        the stones speak a holy name
        and year after year
        the earth proclaims glory and peace
                if only we are of good will.

Listen!
        Something strains to be born
        to shake itself free:
        something brand new trembles
        at the far edge of our minds:
        the shape of a world to come
        conceived in our present labor and pain.

In the distance ahead of us
        people
    of different voice and tone and rhythm
    are gathered in the one great sound
    the life-sound of the future.

Already now
    in our flesh and bone
    we carry blueprints, charts.
The lines each in its proper place
    intersect to form diamonds and prisms
    new patterns of harmony.

Already now
    lifted by the strength of our hope
    we dance
    centered in the music
        in the light
    seeing with new eyes
    singing with new lips:
    PEACE, PEACE, PEACE
the luminous word that was
    in the beginning
        is now
    and ever shall be
in the freedom of our hearts
    word without end:
PEACE, PAIX, PAZ, PAX, SALAAM, SHALOM!

III

Litany of the name of God

LITANY OF THE NAME OF GOD

What is God like ?" asks a child
a question that must wander forever
homeless in a landscape of silence.

BUT
THE NAME OF GOD is sewn in my pocket
a gold coin saved in a time of war.

THE NAME OF GOD is carved on my chest
a seal on my heart, red hot, burning.

THE NAME OF GOD is a piece of paper
stained with tears, scribbled
with words of an unknown tongue.

THE NAME OF GOD dances on the ground
in a thousand feet of joy.

THE NAME OF GOD is a waterfall
crashing down from infinite heights
bursting forth in angel-wings of foam
then pooling gently in the hollows
where women, mothers of the corn
mothers of barley and wheat
wait with empty jars.

THE NAME OF GOD is a round chamber
a womb where the world is born

steaming, luminous, a body
turning in measures of time.

THE NAME OF GOD is tattooed
    on the skin of the lion
    on the membrane of the bat.
    It is threaded through the clouds
    with every ray of light.
    It is the throbbing center
    of all that travels the sky
    day and night in constant spiraling:
    planets, constellations, moons
    and the widespread glittering zodiac
    configurations beyond numbers.

THE NAME OF GOD is the hub
    of time's wheeling sequences
    age upon age of ice, iron and silver
    incised in stone and star.

THE NAME OF GOD flows, energy of the sap
    from root to flower, shaping
    the wild rose full of ecstatic bees.

THE NAME OF GOD is a seed
    buried in depth of plant life
    in mysteries of trees, in the pulse
    of lovers wedded in the hallel of their joy.
    It grows, inviting birth, inventing
    new patterns, new ways to attain
    the moment of ripeness, the fruit.

THE NAME OF GOD bleeds
    in newspapers and magazines:
    Here, in close-up, a dead soldier
    his eyes enormously open; there

a little girl shot in her crib
and further south in the sierras
Indians hung on butcher hooks
tormented for justice' sake.
The face of Christ looks on
through spittle and blood
at the incandescent bloom exploding
over Hiroshima, at the flesh
swollen with plagues, at the minds
invaded by parasites of fear.

What color THE NAME OF GOD
     in Auschwitz, El Salvador, Guatemala
     in Soweto, Tel Aviv and Baghdad?
     Bright red, screaming red
     pouring from the lips of the dying.

In the theatre of the absurd
     THE NAME is seldom spoken:
     the actors eat, walk, sleep
     respond to touch and kiss
     follow signals of simple feelings.
     Sometimes they remember a line
     a lost word of significance
     and THE NAME rises in their throat
     as they plead in urgency, in hunger.

THE NAME OF GOD is a music room
     a cave of resonance filled
     with whistles, whispers, songs
     with choirs of morning birds
     rising crested and feathered
     from the one great egg of creation.
     Voices chant to the eternal reaches
     seldom in harmony, but connected
     word by word of every tongue

speaking the same beloved nouns:
mother father daughter son
sister brother. The sounds
lifted from the four corners
in rhythms, syncopations, drumbeats
mingle high and low, praising.

THE NAME OF GOD is a flying shuttle
weaving, weaving without pause
the broken threads, the pitiful fragments
all the loose, the lost ends, lives
thrown away on the scrap-heap
but retrieved, redeemed, restored
to the loom where the final tapestry
unrolls its luminous sequence.

THE NAME OF GOD is the bronze door
of God's household. On the panels
figures of guardians, prophets and saints
with living faces, living hands
beating hearts. Around the lintel
a vine grows in convoluted branching:
image of life in its timeless leaf and bloom.
From the underworld, grimacing spirits
bring tools forged in darkness.
Their armies obscure the sun
poison the air, ravage the land.
They fail to break the holy door
they retreat, ghosted in their vanishing.

THE NAME OF GOD is a city on fire
and I, within, choke and weep
until I understand: I am called
to be robed and shod in flames
to let my tongue speak hotly
to rejoice in an ardor without end.

THE NAME OF GOD rings
    in all the towers of the world
    a bell to wake the sleepers
    its sound, without angles
    smooth and round in its rolling.
    It enters all dwellings, hovers
    under the eave. It forms itself
    into familiar tones and colors:
    white notes of snow, green of rain
    pastel tinkle of flowers
    golden cracking of thunder.
    Deep in the heart of themselves
    the dreamers hear at the edge of sleep
    the bell's dominant voice
    calling them to the universal feast:
    on the table of the world
    loaves of bread, multiplied and warm.
    It is Easter morning -
        and the bell rings.

IV

the lord's prayer

OUR FATHER WHO ART IN HEAVEN...

Born of sea-water, of blood
we crawl on the beach
    wet, salted with early tears.
Above us, someone screams
    - the mouth of our first world closes.
Our back to the waves, we begin the journey:
    age after age, step after step
        we look for the ancestral home.
Is it here among the lilacs
    a garden where the heart-beat alone
        measures time?
No clock: only a pulse-count, a rhythm
    of moons and tides.
Or is it there, where we follow
    the logic of the hunt:
five hundred years through the continents
    hacking forests
    folding the jungle
        like a green ragged cloth
to come home to a room
    encumbered with machines
to come back
    to the same obsessive search?

Father
    we say Our Father
for we are many
    a tribe dispersed and assembled
        dressed in garments of earth

shirted and shod in this web
        we call flesh. A sorry lot!
All night long we walked down the slopes
        through the junipers and the berry bushes
following one another in time
        son after father, daughter after mother
                carrying speech and skill.
But the past is a distant sound
        a muffled rattling in the ear.
What we said yesterday turns now
        into altered meaning.
We have lost the words
        flicked them off like gnats.
The tower we built, Babel-by-the-Sea
        - metal tongues ringing in a single shell -
                falls to a rusty heap.
From north to south
        the costal towns are visited by plagues:
mushrooms in the rafters
sea-monsters in the wells
        the waters red and soured.

Father
        we have come this way and that
                buzzing with the rest of the swarm
                looking for what? We do not know.
Overhead, the sky curves like a roof:
        it is made of grey stone
                veined in gold and blue.

Father, we pray:
        a gift of sight enters the eye
        and we say: Yes!
In the time of trumpets and drums
        you are
                not the sum of all music

but the one pure silence
in which harmonies are heard.
In the time of darkness, of storm
you are
not sun-king, lord of the rising day
but that one pure source
from which light beyond light
eternally jets forth
to burn into planets and stars.

Father
we believe!

HALLOWED BE THY NAME...

The temple stands four-square
        a place of candles and smoke.
We reach it after the trek
        through desert and grassy plains.
We bang on tambourines and drums
        pluck guitars, ring bells
                - the clap, our will to praise
our metal voice striking
        the metal walls, crying:
                "The temple of God
                        the temple of God
                                the temple of God!"

It is not enough.

There are powers hidden
        in the sap of plants
        in the veins of stones.
There are secrets written
        within the hands
                in these lines long and short
                        criss-crossing the palms:
                a geography of roads
                a map constellated with blood.

We come to the temple dressed and feathered
covered to the eyes
        with all we are not.
We fear to say:

"I am man, I am woman
naked, mortal, dying
        with the long death that begins
                at birth.
What we call life
        is a bluish flame
        sputtering in the dark.
The wick of our days blackens
        the wax melts and drips.

We cannot turn
        cannot forget we are in the flesh
                scarred and suffering;
        cannot reject what is stamped on the mind:
                the dreams of the race
        the eternal delight
                of that rounded body we call earth
                of that glittering star we call sun.

We are children
        of what we see and touch and drink;
we are earthlings
        brother to the fire
        sister to the water
        kin to the lion and the shark.

Father
        to hallow your name
we have words marking time
        rising from the ground of our lives
words for peach-blossom, eyelash, cloud
        for the joining and the parting
        for the coming-as-you-are
                into this place, this temple of everywhere
                        open to the four winds
                where we can say in fleshed spirit

in spiritual flesh:
"HOLY HOLY HOLY
is your name:
FATHER!"

THY KINGDOM COME...

All things move forward, then withdraw:
       the hand, the eyes open and close;
       the word pulled by its own weight
             falls back, returns to silence.

And where are we going?
The wood-demons crack branches
       split logs
       walk heavily on the ground.
They will come, the foresters
       bearing their load
       ready with flint and steel.
And shall it all go up in smoke
       the solid house
       the well-rooted life
       the bright flesh?

We move into the stone of the years
       we chisel, we crack the rock.
In the half-dark of the cave
       voices speak of love, ask questions
             say "How do you do" to strangers
       who answer, "Fine, fine!"
             while death coils itself
                   around their throats.

Where are the kings and queens
       the heirs to the Kingdom?

Children go forth from us
        claiming the moon:
they fill their pockets with moon-chips;
        weightless, suspended among the stars
they dance, they sing in the great void,
        but not for long:
the years stand at their back
        by the thousand
        spelling history and death.
They must return to the room
        where objects are still
        where small lamps give off
                small auras of light.

The Kingdom is within:
        this is the news we learn
                on the stretch of road
                        we travel alone at the latest hour.
Could this be, we wonder
        all there is to find, to cherish, to know?
A dark homeland, a fixed landscape
        the night crunching underfoot like glass?
The Kingdom is within
        deeper than knowledge
                a place beyond all heights and depths.

We come to it, are led to see:
        we own ourselves, we are real;
        we need not fear the wood-demons
                polishing their axes.

"Lord, thy Kingdom is here:
        let us come into its peace!"

THY WILL BE DONE ON EARTH
AS IT IS IN HEAVEN...

Lord, you wrote it
        on the rock and on the tree
        in the lettering of a billion stars
        in the fold of a billion years:
time set upon time, age over age
        the days like pages opened
                to ancient baffling script.
We cannot read it; our eyes are hooded
        with membranes of sleep.
Dreaming, we move into the world
        feeling our way
                through what seems cold and hot
                        dry and wet, sweet and sour.
We sow and reap, our minds scuttle
        through the fields like mechanical reapers
                cutting this and that
                        the cockle and the wheat.
We pack and store:
        winter is always at the door
                a cold beggar, blue-fingered and hungry.
Our cupboards bulge
        our closets are full of facts and fancy.
Yet, when the table is set
        we find only bitter herbs in the dish
                ashes on the water
                dark flakes floating in the cup.

Lord, our flesh dreams softness

dreams silk
        wishes your will easy
to go on the road, traveling easy
        on padded shoes.
Why are the streets iced over?
        Why do we fall in the white morning
                fall awake, roll out of bed
                        into a hard world slicked over
                                with pain?

We look all the way back to the beginning:
        the cave as nursery
        the fire as first guardian
                spirit of the place.
We are sucklings at the breast:
        the earth-mother teaches
                the way of the buffalo
                the manner of the corn.
We are slow movers: we lack skill;
        we live distracted, too pressed
                to feel life living in us
                        - a power of lilac and sun.

Father, let us see
        the full text of your will
as it is here, now
        drawn clear to the inner eye
a thing of beauty
        a power calling us
                to joy.

GIVE US THIS DAY OUR DAILY BREAD...

Clear a field in the mind
        plow deep
make pockets in the ground
        to fill with the seeds of compassion.
Our lives lead nowhere unless they connect
        one to one, one to many;
unless we say: "Take and eat
        this is my own substance.
Drink, this is the spring
        born of caring, the silver strands
                passing through the fingers
                flowing, always on-flowing."

Out of fear, we store, we safe-keep
        while elsewhere actual people die
                propped against thorn-trees
                        near the carcasses of their cows.
Ivory, the bones
        delicately curved
        ideally empty!
The wind blows
        through the eye-sockets
the sand fills the corridors of the skull.

We come awake to the smell of coffee.
The queendom of the kitchen swells
        with colors and scents.
We reach for warm, motherly food
                soft to our soft gums.

The kettle whistles, milk is poured
        the sugar travels through the blood.
Underground, pots and pans
        still black with clinging soot
                lie with ancient dead.

Will today's full cup
        be found in a thousand years, broken
                on the site of a ruined town?
We drip with juices, papaya's, pear's
        the yellow of lemons, the red of berries
                picked at an early hour
                        at the edge of the woods.
But something eludes us, we know not what
        an essential grain, a single kernel.

        Give Us This Day Our Daily Bread
the fat of the land, the corn
        pounded on the stone
the mint, the anise, the fennel and the rue.
        Yes, over the flames, the soup pot
                the roasting meat.
        Yes, in the hands of children
                the sugar-stick, the buttered bread
                        yes!

But more:
        the work has not ended:
we are not so confused as to say
        "Enough, it is enough
                when the dish is full."
There is an ultimate response
        a word we need, a truth
                to feed earth-sucking lips
                to fill our own living hunger
                        that cries and begs:

"Give us today the answer to all seeking:
        here and now
let us sit at the table of the world
        the board rugged
                scratching the resting arms
        but the wine-jars ever filled
                the loaves ever-multiplied
        and our own selves, a space contained
                in space without end.
How real is this? the heart knows
        the pulsing blood speaks.

FORGIVE US OUR TRESPASSES...

Look at us, soft-gathered
    around a trembling center:
can we be anything but wanderers
    changelings pressed
        by time-changes, body-changes
           through places of drift and flux?
So, over and again
    "Farewell, sweet prince!"
We fold our tent, move on
    through the rise and fall
        the dust of hazy hills.

Look at us: we hang in orbit
    weightless.
We have made it
    the impossible journey
    the visit to the Sea of Tranquility
        to the waterless bed.
Ah, for what? In her lighted temple
    the moon calls for rituals
        pulls our tides
           with implacable hands.

Ah, for what?
We do not even know
    the stranger dwelling in our clothes
        living our life, dying our death.
We are shadows of shadows
    children of the dark side of the street.

Our own secrets are hidden:
        we see only by earth-light
        we struggle to keep ourselves awake
                attuned to gravity
                in power.

Have pity on us who are pitiful!
        Yes, we bottle our tears.
        Yes, we flaunt our wounds.
We are babes in a deep wood
        wailing for Mama
                big, beautiful Mama
                        with sugar-breasts
                                and arms like warm pillows!

Have mercy on us who are sinners!
        In us, through vast dream-plains
powerful animals are hunting.
        Wild beyond caution, they run
                fitting our bodies to their wishing.
Hands unshape themselves
        slip into fur and claw;
jaws grow huge: caverns of appetite
        hungering for meat.

Instructed by dark beasts, we hunt
        sweeping across the earth
        leveling cities
        pouring salt on good fields
        ripping the forests open.
The beasts stir in us:
        they wear our faces like masks.

Lord, have mercy on us now
        and at the hour of our death!

AS WE FORGIVE THOSE WHO
TRESPASS AGAINST US...

Our eyes burn
    so intensely they see
        that one Man:
He lies stretched over the continents
    scarlet threads are pulled
        through his hands and feet;
his limbs drip blood over Asia
his open wrists pour over South America
    the wounds in his back ooze
        over the night-lands where we struggle.

We touch cold iron in the dark:
    stove without fire, pot without meat
    water-pipes dry and rusty.
Who has done this to us
    taken away the sweet rain
        the bounding deer
        the oil and the coal?
Why do we starve?
Why, why, why do we thirst?

"Forgive," he says
    "learn the difficult skill!"
Can we shake the bees of anger
    stinging the memory
    pumping venom in the mind?
Can we forget the hooks, the ropes
    the dangling lures - little mirrors
        in which we lost our way?

He bleeds over cities and fields:
        large drops fall, pool in the cracks.
"Drink that wine," he says
        "drink the power of mercy!"
We let it flow within.

Heavy, they are stone-heavy
        those we carry.
The very smell of their clothes
        their very touch
                fill us with revulsion.
They have driven us in chains
        across water-miles;
they have herded us like cattle
        they have kicked us
                broken our teeth
- we speak through wired jaws
        see through gauzy patches;
we walk on crutches
        but we carry them
                our brothers, our sisters;
we hold them who need to be held
        in pardon and mercy.

For millions of years
        cycle after cycle
                the moon has risen full;
for millions of years
        life on this planet pulses
                waxes and wanes like the moon.
All things fall to fatten the soil
        but that one presence remains:
that one risen Man saying, "Peace
        love your enemy
do good to those who hate you
        forgive
                and you shall be forgiven."

LET US NOT FALL INTO TEMPTATION...

They are so many:
    creatures of the deep
            rising sweet-voiced
            lifting themselves
                    out of the waves
    illusions caught in scales and fins.

We have come to the sea-mouth:
    the air stinks of fish.
On the beach,
        the jelly of the dying medusa
                shivers blue and green.
At our back, the land grows ripe
        the fruit hang in the trees:
plum, apple, the succulence of flesh
        belonging to others: we cannot touch!
Before us, the liquid mother
        filled with froth, full of food
                glutted.

We sit on the sand
        hear beyond the laughing gulls
                the sound of plucked strings: lute?
Ancient music drifts in the wind
        floods us with longing;
thousands of hands finger our clothes
        tug at the hem of our coat;
nails lightly scratch our naked throat;
        we are hot;
we fear what lives in the mind

that trapped power within the skull
        that monster ready to tear
            to thieve, to kill.
We, it is we whose faces appear
        in the comic books:
                dwarfs and giants
                mermaids and mermen
        lifting themselves - raw, untender -
                from the pages
        chanting their sad song.

If that pain were to last
        and anger not lie down
                like a dog exhausted
                        from too much barking
and if lust were not to break itself
        - an earthen cup
                flung against eternal rocks -
        then what?

The old stories are about death:
        they repeat themselves.
Year after year
        they bring images of boats
                sailing dark on darkening waters
                sailing down around the capes
                        where perpetual winds blow
                                full-cheeked
                                        spinning the hulls mad.

Father, lead us away from the bitter waters
        from the home of turbulent spirits
into a garden, a place of hushed voices
        where tamed beasts lie on flagstones
                their golden eyes, half closed
                in deep rest!

Father, no more raging
        no more bonfires over which to leap
        no more rocking by the sea-mother
- she wept in our tears
        called from the very salt in our blood.
No more!
        Receive us in your peace!

BUT DELIVER US FROM EVIL...

Deliver us from the evil
        that grins through the teeth
                glows through the slit of the eye.
Yes, we shall spit it out
        we shall weep ardent tears
                say we regret - but again and again
we find ourselves surprised:
        in the dark of the mind
        in the cave
murderous words crouch and wait.

We make, we destroy;
        weapons are stockpiled
        bombs hang like eggs
                in the claws of the soaring eagle.
We give birth, sing lullabies:
        elsewhere, we kill the child
crossing the footbridge
        in the wrong time in a year of war.

Deliver us from evil!

Legions, they are legions:
        like horsemen, they ride in the wind
                dressed in steel shells
                clanging with spurs and swords.
They rip through the pages of history
        stuff the word "death" into time's cracks
        spreading foul scents over the land.

There are radiant faces lightly borne
        on long-stemmed bodies:
flowering girls
        shining young men.
But the monstrous army comes in
        bitter-strong, whipping the lights out.
Voices in the city
        a running of voices
        a bleeding of sounds!
Why are mothers with leaking breasts
        weeping?
Why are babies still?

Deliver us:
        it is late in the day
near evening maybe on the cosmic clock
        - centuries are minutes
                raining into space.
What have we done all time long?
        Sold what belonged to others?
        Chosen cowardly silence?
        Forsaken the poor?

Deliver us from evil:
        from the glut and the smell
                of bulging cupboards
                of closets where we store
                        more than we need.
Turn the mind, that strange stone
        to the fire-light of your truth.
Let us invent something new
        a new way of seeing, of knowing, of being.
Let us begin
        to be human!

FOR THINE IS THE KINGDOM
AND THE POWER AND THE GLORY.

We move by sight, by touch
        in enormous rooms.
Rivers and seas lap at the threshold:
        what do we know?
Six hundred generations
        since the Egyptians:
how many since the raw beginning
        since the yolk of life oozed
                into the blank void?

The time-clock ticks on
        recording wars, death-marches
                plagues and famines.
Onward we go, moving by touch
        by sight
bumping into the furniture:
        the towers we built
        the temples on the hills
        the columns, altars and thrones.
We are many, we are alone
        we walk deeper into the cold
- it is winter on the plains:
        a new ice-age stills the waters
                freezes the flames.
We shiver, isolated machines
        engines pumping heat
                to the surface of the skin.

Father, we need you
        we call from the distance where we crouch:
small men and women lost
        in great cavernous depths.
Our words echo ancient runes
        retell ancestral lore.
Figures on the wall leap
        as in a dance
            run with antlered beasts.
We are the same people
        image-makers, hunters
        inventors of the fire;
we call you with one voice
        from these enormous rooms
            where the sound rubberballs
                from moment to moment
                from century to century
                    repeating:
                    THINE IS THE KINGDOM
                    AND THE POWER
                    AND THE GLORY!

V

a time for everything

A TIME FOR EVERYTHING

*There is a season for everything, a time
for every occupation under heaven:*

*A time for giving birth,
a time for dying;
a time for planting,
a time for uprooting what has been planted.
A time for killing,
a time for healing;
a time for knocking down,
a time for building.
A time for tears,
a time for laughter;
a time for mourning,
a time for dancing.
A time for throwing stones away,
a time for gathering them up;
a time for embracing,
a time to refrain from embracing.
A time for searching,
a time for losing;
a time for keeping,
a time for throwing away.
A time for tearing,
a time for sewing;
a time for keeping silent,
a time for speaking.
A time for loving,
a time for hating;
a time for war,
a time for peace.*

Ecclesiastes, 3:1-8

A TIME FOR GIVING BIRTH

This creature breaking open
        her hands clamped to cold steel
        - bed-frame, dangerous cliff
                at the edge of the world -
this woman dwells at the center:
        time in pulsing rays
                streams from her womb.

Yesterday she knelt by the river
        collecting duck eggs;
yesterday she pounded grain:
        she the stony bowl
                curved under the pestle
        she the crushed corn.

Last winter she could be seen
        walking through the forest:
a bent figure in a cage of trees
        goddess of no leisure
                gathering firewood.
Later, in a furnished room
        her legacy forgotten
she stood before a mirror
        curling her hair.

Now everything is laid aside:
        clothes, habits, speech
all that ties her to a name
        to a place.

She is the mother-image
        stamped on the clay;
she is Eve at the beginning
        holding the sequel of ages
                the raw lump of history
        encapsulated in her flesh.

In her skull, pain detonates
        its thousand burning flares.
She strains
        - it is too late to ask
                how these bones are unlocking.
She screams.
        Silent, eyes closed
the child bursts forth
        into enormous space
        into terrible inescapable light.

A TIME FOR DYING

Released
    from its habitual sequence
time settles for small details
    for moments barely moving
        along the rim of the day.
What was solid, sharp, defined
    - tree, bedframe, cup -
turns soft, becomes a pulpy mass.
We notice in limb and heart
    a feeling unlike any other
of being lighter, airborne
    like winged seed lifted by the wind.

The earth continues to breathe
    - business as usual in root and leaf;
words continue to be added
    to the endless chain of stories
        that circles the globe.
But inside the skull
    images fade
    the particular shades
    the tones of perceptions dim.

It is snowing in the interior:
    a fine silvery powder
    layers the map of private landscapes
    blurs the contours of what was known.
Soon nothing remains but swirling flakes
    falling in absolute silence.

The very absence of sound
        becomes an immense vibration
            a shattering power.
All the crystals of life
        - window-panes, mirrors
            the ice of accumulated winters -
crack and scatter in brilliant pieces.

When the debris are cleared
        we stand in the open
            in the streaming light.

A TIME FOR PLANTING

Searching beyond the end of memory
   in what seems to be a leafy tangle
my hand closes around a fat pod:
the nail, pressing on the seam
opens the jewel-box of seeds.
Overhead, a great bronze sun hangs
     immense, prehistoric
        in empty morning skies.
Long ago, the mind learned
   the source of the color green
hidden in the wrinkled fruit
   at the core where thoughts break
      to release names, words
        a syntax of life.

Now the earth, that holy shelter
   that lovely rough coat I used to wear
      loose and easy from the shoulders
stiffens into a frozen cloak.
I am alone in the granary
   dipping my arms in the golden heap
   knowing what fire sleeps, locked
      in these hard pebbles, these seeds.

It is time: I enter
   the darkness of roots:
No other light but the will to grow
   the passion to survive.

I plant these small orbs
        set these letters in neat rows.
Later, on damp spring days
        they shall bear green antennas
              rise on trembling stems
              speak a modest truth.

A TIME FOR UPROOTING

Inch by inch, they slithered under the porch
    blind snakes of roots
        their movements unseen
        their grip powerfully lifting
            the mind's foundation.
They are the invaders, the aliens
    ready to crack the walls
        to expose our lives, ourselves
            to the wind, to the driven snow.

Yes, years ago we planted these saplings
    these thoughts;
we only asked for growth
    waited for the green pleasure of leaves
        for patterns couched on the ground
            in light and shadow.
At first, we welcomed the spreading branches
    the emerald image of the tree.
We did not know: below the surface
    roots were sending giant probes
        working to find the place
            of eroding certitude
            of lesser hope.

It is time to save ourselves
    prune the trees of the imagination
    push the wilderness back
leaving open spaces
    room for the language
        of air and sun.

A TIME FOR KILLING

A winter of wild swans
- two of them flying low
float over the treetops
becoming as they pass
more and more necessary
to our morning lives.
BUT NO!
This is not a time for poetry
for pacific birds landing in the marshes.
The evidence exists: here and there
in certain hidden spots
the harvest grows:
pyramids of bones
monuments of teeth.

In the living room
we breathe the scent of burning pine
eat oranges and pears
chat while centuries of terror flow
by our doorstep.
Their dark fluid seeps under the sill
stains the floor.

Outside, the wind bangs
against the house
making deep wooden sounds.
We glance through the window:
no one on the road but death
a purple heart sewn to his chest
marching to yet another endless war.

A TIME FOR HEALING

Battered, numb
>   our need whittled to sharp pain
>   we wait.
Questions form themselves:
>   hard, ripe buds ready to release
>   their useless green flags.

Out of what land were we driven
>   swimming what river
>   carrying what child
>   away from preying beasts?
No longer do we know: the images
>   forever printed on the retina
>   bear no sign of place, no date.
But the bruises
>   - a million years in the making -
>   are purple-black and throbbing.
Swollen limbs ache
>   broken fingers, burned skin
contradict
>   the clean brightness of the day.

In the ancient cave
>   fur beds, deep as dreams, await us.
We cannot go back: voices call
>   hands pull us into the future
>   out of lime-pits and leaky boats
>   out of hospital cots
>   out of centuries of hunger.

We come forth: behind us
        the rolled stone
        the mess of linens
                soaked with myrrh and blood;
before us, the sun breaks
        through a thin line of trees
changing the texture of our lives
        from dark-stitched coarseness
                to the silken ease of light.

A TIME FOR KNOCKING DOWN

Stripped of its grey bones
	the house is empty now
		a shell filled by the wind
			with deep oceanic sounds.
Nothing left but ghosts
	huddled in corners
velvety shadows
	blown from room to room.
Once they had faces
	spoke among themselves
		using words we still understand:
			bread, candle, firewood.
Their message reaches us:
	we hear our name repeated
		handed over in caress
			in blessing
		from one mother to the next.

Time to turn away
	to let the house die.
Shall its soul escape
	in the shape of a weeping woman
		lifting long heavy skirts
			as she runs from her loss?

Young, cheerful
	the workmen have arrived
		driving their wrecking machines
			over the ancient flower-beds.

When the iron ball strikes the wall
our heart booms in its cave
breaks with the roof
burying a hundred years of care
under rubble and dust.

A TIME FOR BUILDING

They rest upon her shoulders
    layers of stone
    layers of wood.
She opens her arms
    her strong hands
        to hold a floor of rough planks.
Over her eyes
    a great faceted room shines
        with many windows facing the sun.
Cupboards slam their doors
    over her mouth.
She is silent, but her children sing
    of butterflies and roses.
Squat on tired haunches
    she hears the earth crying
with the voice of what is chained:
    voice of roots, of ancient trees
    voice of captured waters
        flowing in iron pipes.
She does not mind
    endures constraint, changes:
night and day
    the passing of seasons altering her looks.
Not for her goodbyes and farewells:
    she lives at the center
        keeper of fire and lamp
        mother of seeds
        house of bread.

A TIME FOR TEARS

They exist only on human faces:
hard crystals melting in the heat
flowing luminescent
    over the hills of cheeks
        bitter to the tongue.
They are wiped off
    with the back of the hand
    with an apron's corner
    with pieces of rag.
At other times, they stream unattended
    along slopes of cold flesh
spilling from great urns of sorrow
    from stone jars of pain.
Formed in the underground
    at the juncture of bones
        in ducts where grief is mined
they are brought to the glare
    of another day.

A time for weeping:
    any time will do:
        mornings of accidents
        evenings of earthquakes
        nights when the gutted candle
            speaks forth
        one last desperate word of light.
See the holy dead:
    they who were taken
        in the act of making bread

of running, of sleeping
in weakness, in strength.

They glide on rivers of tears
    are carried to salty seas
where memory sets them on fire
    to return them clarified
        defined by the unction of love.
A time for weeping:
    any time here on earth.

A TIME FOR LAUGHTER

For my grandson David, age two,
because the first word I heard him say was "flower."

The child adjusts breath
     to tongue and lips
shapes the sound
     of his first word:
"Flower," he says, reaching
     for the place on the south wall
where the morning-glory
     opens its deep blue doors.

In what honeycomb of the brain
     did the bees of memory store
          the data for pollen and petals?
In the beginning, when cells assembled
     to form rootlet, stem and bud
did they, too, hold joy
     the laughter of the man-child
as his eyes meet and correspond
     - blue for blue -
with the morning beauty
     the climber to the sun
          on the south wall?

A TIME FOR MOURNING

From the heart of stones
 a wailing sound arises
  low at first, then amplified.
Is it the wind
 tipping over the rock tables
 tilting the sky
 sucking the dust
  into whirlpools?
The procession goes by
 men in black suits
 women with shawls
  wrapped tight
   around their shoulders.

Someone is being carried away
 the only son of a mother
 the once child
who suckled breasts
 now older and dry.
There are no flowers
 no candles
only the pierced body of this Man
 redolent with ointments and herbs.
Around him, the earth spins
 in dust and high wind.
"Even the stones," he said
 would cry out his praise.
Now they split open
 bleeding their one long scream
  through the coming night.

A TIME FOR DANCING

No one can guess
    the traffic of our thoughts
all these railway cars moving
    silently on invisible tracks
transporting memories
    to safe distant caves.
No one can guess how we journey
    through unknown lands
      deep in the dream of ourselves
to find a clearing
    a smooth empty space
where suddenly we can hear
    undulating in the wind
      a faint musical phrase.
And hearing it, we know
    this is the time of jubilation
the place where the lion
    eats straw with the lamb
- all tearing having ended
    all blood ceased to flow
      from terribly opened wounds.
No one can guess
    how we rise then
- our body radiant with energy
    our limbs oiled with strength -
and dance
    centered in the music
      in the light.

A TIME FOR THROWING STONES AWAY

Every stone cracked or chipped
      every one knocked down
           by the picks of the demolition crew.
Long ago, they had been hauled
      out of the ground
blunt-cut, then fitted to each other
      until some shape was reached
of a grey house brooding
      over a landscape of rough fields.

Now the stones are thrown away
      heaped into rockpiles
to be covered with lichen
      with lattice of wild grass.

In some distance of years
      they may be found and numbered
coaxed into revealing
      what they had sheltered in the past:
voices saying lamb, bread, apple
      in a foreign tongue;
lives of ancestors fallen to dust
      but once strong, bone-hard
their emblems - fingerprints and smoke -
      forever deep-set in the rock.

A TIME FOR GATHERING STONES

In their veins
    they hold the hard evidence:
        time beyond count
        secret beginnings
        negotiated without us
            through darkness and fire.

Here they are: grey eggs of stone
    set on the beach for another eternity
        of being solidly enclosed
            sealed into their own reality
                of stillness, of silence.

How fragile, how dangerously exposed
    the hand that gathers them!
We who shall not endure
    but are warm with thought and blood
haul these cold rocks
    to build a little altar:
witness to our presence
    to our power of praise.

A TIME FOR EMBRACING

When you come in, the room expands:
    I hear the walls cracking open
        the roof detonating
    lifted by the explosion of your power.
You bring me good news,
    tell me that calendars lie
that clocks need not ring
    the change of each day.
Even death, that trap-door
    concealed under the rug
can be stepped over without risk
    of landing in the dark.

How long I waited!
    Cold, without comfort
I had gathered the floss of winter
    woven the snow into blankets and shawls.
When you entered the room
    they melted in my hands;
violets broke through the floor
    trees draped the windows
        with green and lacy cloth.

Now, when you appear
    I cannot form syllables and sounds
        the simple words for arms, eyes, mouth
but I clasp you, hold you
    in a place of permanence
        farther, deeper than time.

A TIME TO REFRAIN
FROM EMBRACING

Behind me on the trail
    a litter of collapsed years
broken gunny sacks
    spilling hard pebbles of words.
The past is used up: goodbye, then
    good night!

This place throbbed with sounds
    with the boom and slosh of life.
I have heard it all, the song
    of water, air, fire
    of this lovely loam
      sonorous with the work of roots.

Enough now: it is time to leave
    the embrace of mortal arms
    the velvet kiss of life!
I am shedding my life
    like a coat of feathers
transforming myself to fit
    the currents and passages
      between cloud and star.

Come, my Falcon, my Hunter!
    Weightless, willing, I wait
a prey to be quick-lifted
    through the breaking mirror of the sun.

A TIME FOR SEARCHING

See you around
    the curve of the earth
where the ocean dips and falls
    in sheets of white waters.
To a city beneath the waves
    I return
to a sunken drowned house
    searching the rooms now alive
      with the motions of algae and fish.
Crystals of sand and salt
    fill the cups on the table.
The once familiar chairs
    float in blue darkness.
Holding my breath, I look for you
    plunging deeper and deeper
    swimming through tunnels of time.
Nothing remains in the vaults
    but stones rubbed soft
      by patient water-hands.
I call your name: the sound of it
    disturbs the order of the past
    stirs the sediments of memory.
You cannot answer:
    in the stained photographs
your eyes are black holes
    empty caverns I cannot enter.

A TIME FOR LOSING

I detach myself from myself:
        face fading in the mirror
        image peeled from the retina.
I move away inch by inch
        slowly discarding my treasures:
silver spoon to eat
        the white pap of time;
combs to pass through the hair
        of dream animals;
cloth of many colors
        to stitch and quilt around my life
                into padded layers of isolation.

Gone from me my childhood
        deep in buttercups and bruises;
lost the years that were poured
        steaming in unbreakable bowls:
oatmeal for the children
        soup for hungry passers-by.
Yet I remain, my bones well counted
        exactly placed in their cage of flesh;
my heart alive, my mouth full of penny-words
        - all the silver ones spent
                forever stuck in slot machines.
I am poor now
        walk in a new land of perception
                of knowledge:
light, my footsteps
        noiseless on the iron
                of the frozen world.

A TIME FOR KEEPING

What part of time, what hour
    shall we choose
- a talisman to keep -
    before we leave
    before we run up the ramp
      of the waiting ark?
Water already laps the sill
    licking our feet with icy wet tongue.

What shall we take along?
    Diagrams of houses charged
      with the weight of our living?
    Figures of the moon
      their numbers rolling
        through the heavens
          in silver hoops?
Or shall we pick up these shoes
    this dress that hangs in the closet
      grey and limp
    like a lizard's sloughed skin?

As the sky darkens
    and rain drowns the land
we shall carry
    cupped in our hands
a small steady flame
    light of remembrance
      of worship
      of praise.

A TIME FOR THROWING AWAY

You see it can be done:
    clean the floor
    sweep the cave
where the bones of extinct species
    rot and stink.
Take out the old litter
    frayed language
    words raveled beyond mending.
Get rid of the souvenirs:
    medals and helmets
    guns polished
        by speeches and spit.
With great care
    watching your steps
carry out the explosives
    contentions, lies, every sound
        ready to detonate and kill.

We are right on schedule:
    look at the trees sticky
        with the glue of new buds.
True to the images we had kept
    locked in our winter mind
plants lift leafy stems
    cup themselves into amazing bloom:
tulips and primroses
    chain-linked to other gardens
        other springs.

It is time to crawl out of our woolly shell
        to push away the weight:
            wraps and shawls
            husks of thoughts
                certified and sealed.
We wake to a new age
        laid out like a map
            we must study and enter.

A TIME FOR TEARING

Rip the seams
    tear the great web
    the net in which we are caught.
Language wove itself around us
    word by word
    loop by patient loop
until we suddenly discovered
    we were locked in
    entangled in the threads.

They lied to us
    the soft-rounded phrases
        copied over and again
        from manuals of war.
Too late did we notice
    they were containers of plague
        carriers of burning phosphorus
        arsenals glittering with guns.

It is time to hack our way out
    through the rusted wires.
The steel barbs enter our hands
    our palms bleed
but we break through
    dare to invent new sounds
        a vocabulary that fits us
        that flows around our lives
            in wild billowing folds
                supple as water
                and free.

A TIME FOR SEWING

Cotton, taffeta, wool
    we choose according to the season
    to the mood.
At arms length
    we hold yards of satin
to drape around our feelings
    our thoughts.

How luminous we become:
    women of beauty
    vessels of poetry and fable.
Yet it is our own same selves
    seated hour by hour at the window
    piecing together patches of time
    pulling blunt needle, coarse thread
        through ill-matched scraps.

Often it seems we are wearing
    whatever is on hand:
scarf of hours casually tied
    around our hair;
apron to catch spill and drip.

But in our minds, always, we unroll
    bolts of silk
we cut and clip and stitch
    ample robes
under which we feel petaled like roses
    women of allure and wit.

Now November chills the air:
        it is time to reach for warmth
            - down of arctic bird
            hair of the llama;
it is time to work
        to sew a lifetime of years
into cloud-like quilts
        to pull over our rigid form.

A TIME FOR KEEPING SILENT

Doors closed, shades drawn, eyes shut
        I cross over that territory
                mapped long ago
a place of no words, no sounds.
At first
        on the waterways of the mind
the traffic moves at a furious pace:
        thoughts gun their engines
                bounce across the field of vision.
They are replaced by slower gondolas
        gliding like elegant swans
                toward the horizon line
                        where they tip over and vanish.

Soon a new flotilla comes in sight:
        bulky rowboats
                carrying provisions and fuel
their oars noisily cutting
        through the gathering quiet.
They too disappear
        leaving the surface of the river
                grey and neutral
        a mirror without reflections.
Now I stand in pure emptiness:
        the waters freeze
                turn to crystals, to ice.
In a time-flash
        - a day or a thousand years -
I enter the silence where light silently thunders.

A TIME FOR SPEAKING

Between two worlds
       we stand accused
              of disturbing the symmetry of darkness.
We run through the maze
       beaming our flashlights
              on centuries of rubble.
Faces lifted from the night
       look up
their eyes deep-set in the skull
       their mouths drawn in red ink
              spitting teeth and blood.

It would be easy to sink back
       into the silk of our ease
forget the commonplace of pain:
       houses exploding in the distance
       children growing wings of flame
       fugitives drowning with their leaky boats.

But history burns in the cloud:
       what falls out
are names of cities and towns
       a snow of flesh
       a powder of bones.
The time of our own death
       is written down
              stamped on tickets
                     folded in our purse.
We scour the ruins

       seek the golden glint
of good words
     find nothing
but a terrible scream
      a buried voice pleading for peace.

A TIME FOR LOVING

not when the moon hangs
    its luminous silk
        above the maple;
not when the bed is freshly made
    the sheets taken off the line
        still warm from the sun;
but when the surface is disturbed
    of that body of water, of ease
I navigate on clear days;
    when the cost of a single word
goes up
    becomes an incredible sum
spelling bankruptcy, dismissal
    eviction into the streets:
then, yes, it is time to love
    to say, "Yes
I will shoulder the burden
    weep these tears
        die this death!"

A TIME FOR HATING

What can we say
when on the screen of the mind
        these figures appear:
ragged, hollow-eyed, trudging
        through snowy plains?
What can we feel
knowing women are chained
        to stony walls in caves of despair?
We need to live
        through the final radiation
to come out at the other end of fear.

We crawled for so long
        through that tunnel
        our knees bleeding
        our souls scraped raw.
Can hate burn away the evidence:
        bone-fragments, skulls
        found at the foot of the cliff?
Can hate suppress that white pain
        that fire of compassion
        pulsing under the ribs
                like a wound?

We search for remedy
        scour the hills for healing herbs
        pound our best thoughts
        in the mortar of truth.
We are left with a mess

stinking of wild onions
        of plants decayed by long rains.
What will happen to us
        when the ebb-tide of violence
        pulls us with iron claws?
Shall we then release
        the cries trapped in our throats
- these magpies, these crows -
        to announce our anger?
Or shall we lie down in gentleness
        and say: "No, we cannot hate:
that hour will never strike
that time will never come."

A TIME FOR WAR

Like tissue-paper pulled apart
        the city begins to tear
                noiselessly, street by street.
Before they fall
        the houses wear crests
                of brilliant flames.
Many eyes open in the glare
        explode in the heat.
Bodies of men, of women
        float out of broken doors
        turn to droplets of dust
                carried by poisonous air.

The tablets and scrolls
        the messages painted in gold leaf
have been lifted on high
        to be returned, to snow down
- a blizzard of confetti
        over the boiling river
each particle, each flake
        a dying word, a last greeting.

No enemy is visible;
        no one comes to claim the land:
only darkness
        and an army of guardian stones
stand watch, witness
        the time of the end.

A TIME FOR PEACE

We can still make it
        gather the threads, the pieces
each of different size and shape
        to match and sew into a pattern:
Rose of Sharon
        Wedding Rings
                Circles and Crowns.

We can still listen: children at play
        their voices mingling
                in the present tense
                        of a time that can be extended.

What do we want, after all?
The pasture next door
        where the unicorn grazes
        its horn deep in sweet blue grass?
Or our own weedy yard
        with its old trees
                its modest plot
where people stretch in the sun
        on Sunday afternoons?

Peace we say, looking through our pockets
        to find the golden word
                the coin to buy that ease
                        that place sheltered
                                from bullets and bombs.
But what we seek lies elsewhere

beyond the course of lethargic blood
beyond the narrow dream
        of resting safe and warm.

If we adjust our lenses
        we see far into the distance
                figures of marching people
                        homeless, hungry, going nowhere.
Why not call them
        to our mornings of bread and milk?

The coming night will be darker
        than the heart of stones
unless we strike the match
        light the guiding candle
        say, "Yes, there is room after all
                at the inn."

VI

the oliver poems

The story of Oliver is told by his brother, Christopher de Vinck,
in the book: THE POWER OF THE POWERLESS
(New York: Doubleday, 1988).

FOR MY SON OLIVER
(April 20, 1947 - March 12, 1980)

keep still:
    The word "death" forms itself
    - a bubble in your mouth -
    pushes itself clear
    through your lips
    screams red into the room.

It is noon: time is a hurled stone
    a meteor of unknown substance
falling fast, shattering
    the glass shell of the mind.
A splinter of hard brilliance
    finds, under the breastbone
    the trembling place: my heart.

Once more, I lean over
    kiss your face.
Your body now a glacial ridge
    a mystery
removes itself at increased speed
    further and further away from me.

Perspectives shift
    alter the March light
as it pours, milky white
    through the window.
The trees, polished by the sun
    shine like tin

the same trees
    seen yesterday less sharply.

From the fixed ground of your dying
    I hear the sound of working roots
of seeds breaking open to release
    stems of greening life.
Now your limbs slip out
    of icy winter wraps;
now the scaly buds of your eyes
    open into iris-blue flowers
and you wake to sight never seen
    as I return to strict necessity
to a world of doors and clocks
    of banked fires sending out
    feeble messages, sparks and smoke.

THE BURIAL
(May 17, 1980, at the Priory in Weston, Vermont.)

They are burying
    the small treasure of his hands
    the bread of his flesh
    now hard and stale.

The earth is open:
    a gash, bleeding stones and sand.

I am
    alive by the grave
feel my mouth warm and moist
    - the tongue moving in its cave
    forming words, taming
    what wildly circulates in the blood
    the scream of all that dies in pain.

    They are letting him down.

How easily the cargo of his years
    slips into the underground.
On the river of the dead
    the oarsman is masked;
his dog barks silently
    in the shadows.

I am aware of the body:
    beneath my dress
my limbs, my breasts

the central place of the womb.
I imagine the darkness within
        the soft pillowed place
where yesterday the child hung
        ripe, heavy as a pod.

Between time and time
        life is ground fine
        a powder of ashes and roses.

I do not weep:
        this hole is empty
        but for tree-roots and bones.

Lord of the Living
        receive my son!

VII

REQUIEM
FOR THE
CHILDREN OF IRAQ

REQUIEM
FOR THE CHILDREN OF IRAQ

From the dark body of the earth
    tears flow in huge rivers;
    furious winds churn the sky
    rip branches from the mother-tree.
Death, a hag in gaudy dress
    walks the land claiming her spoils:
    victory by fire, victory by guns
    victory by hunger and thirst.

No longer will they dream, the children
    of days like oriental carpets
    woven with birds and flowers.
No longer will they soar, the little ones
    on the bright wings of their hopes.
They are buried under rubble
    their skull broken, their spine twisted
    the delicate bridge of their ribs
    crushed under mortar and stone.

In the curve of sounds
    arching over the world
cries rise, cries that nothing can stop
    like blood pouring from ruptured veins.
Bitter, bitter the mouths
    opened to that crying; they thirst
    for cool water, for tender words.

The mothers, with leaking breasts
        weep, sail on the river of sorrow
        downhill toward the salted sea.

VIII

hope

HOPE

now that life itself is flattened
    pierced by nails, wreathed in thorns
now that your own body falls
    soft and limp into empty space
- nothing to catch, no foothold
    no ledge
only white emptiness
    through which you descend:
the ground comes closer
    the hard stony earth looms larger.
Already you imagine your bones broken
    your hands useless, you life crushed.
Just before you are to hit rock-bottom
    a small parachute of hope opens
    a corolla with filaments of light
and you are held, you swing free
    from deadly gravity:
you float in azure currents
    through lanes of air
through wide avenue of pure ozone
    and go on living another day.

THREE THOUSAND COPIES

typeset by MK Design

in 13 & 11 point Times Roman and Italics

with Libra Titles

and Munch dotted capitals

printed and bound by

THOMSON-SHORE of Dexter, MI.

constitute the

ORIGINAL EDITION.